Weaving Wonders

spiders in Your Backyard

by Nancy Loewen

illustrated by Rick Peterson

Thanks to our advisers for their expertise, research, knowledge, and advice:

Blake Newton, Extension Entomologist
University of Kentucky

Susan Kesselring, M.A., Literacy Educator
Rosemount–Apple Valley–Eagan (Minnesota) School District

PICTURE WINDOW BOOKS
Minneapolis, Minnesota

Editorial Director: Carol Jones
Managing Editor: Catherine Neitge
Creative Director: Keith Griffin
Editor: Jill Kalz
Story Consultant: Terry Flaherty
Designer: Nathan Gassman
Page Production: Picture Window Books
The illustrations in this book were created with acrylics.

Picture Window Books
5115 Excelsior Boulevard
Suite 232
Minneapolis, MN 55416
877-845-8392
www.picturewindowbooks.com

Printed in the United States of America.

Library of Congress Cataloging-in-Publication Data
Loewen, Nancy, 1964–
Weaving wonders : spiders in your backyard / by Nancy Loewen ; illustrated by
Rick Peterson.
p. cm. — (Backyard bugs)
ISBN 1-4048-1145-1 (hardcover)
1. Spiders—Juvenile literature. I. Peterson, Rick, ill. II. Title.
QL458.4.L64 2006
595.4'4—dc22
                                                                2005004061

Table of Contents

Creepy-Crawly Friends

Eeeek! Look over there, on the shed. It's a spider!

Do you think spiders are creepy? A lot of people do. But, creepy or not, spiders are actually very helpful. They eat lots of pesky bugs.

Spiders live all over the world. Some are as tiny as the head of a pin, while others are bigger than an adult's hand.

Spiders are also food for birds,
frogs, lizards, and other animals.

This little guy isn't going to hurt anyone. Let's take a closer look.

How many legs does this spider have? That's right—eight. A spider is often called a bug, but it's not. Bugs have six legs and three main body parts, while spiders have eight legs and two main body parts.

Spiders bite people only in self-defense. Their bite is usually harmless. Of the thousands of kinds of spiders, only a few have venom powerful enough to make a person ill.

Weaving Webs

What is that thing in the corner? It must be a spider's web. Many spiders make webs to catch food.

Different kinds of spiders
make different kinds of webs.
The webs you're most likely
to see inside your house are
called cobwebs. They're usually
covered with dust and dirt. Outside,
you might find large, ball-shaped webs
with beautiful designs.

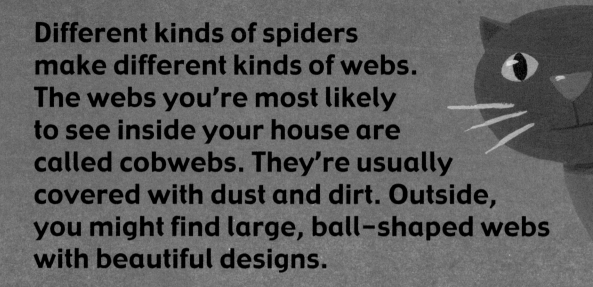

Only about half of all
spiders make webs to
trap food. The others
hunt for their prey, or
wait for prey to come
to them.

How does a spider make a web? First, the spider's body makes liquid silk. The liquid passes through one, two, or three pairs of spinnerets. Spinnerets are body parts located at the tip of the spider's abdomen.

Using its back legs, the spider pulls out the silk. The silk quickly hardens, and the spider shapes it into a web.

Spider silk is very strong and more stretchy than nylon.

13

A Liquid Lunch

Most spider webs are very sticky. When bugs fly into the webs, the bugs become trapped.

Some spiders paralyze their prey with venom. Other spiders wrap their prey in silk.

Next, the spider spits digestive juices into the bug. The bug's insides turn into liquid, and the spider sucks the liquid out.

Not all parts of a spider's web are sticky. The spider knows which parts aren't sticky and uses them when climbing.

Laying Eggs

When you see a lot of spiders around, it's probably mating season. Male spiders are out looking for females.

Before mating, the male plucks on the female's web or does a special dance. After mating, he must hurry away—or the female might eat him.

After mating, the female spider lays eggs in a little egg case made of silk. Some kinds of spiders guard their cases. Others carry them around.

Spiders, Spiders Everywhere

Now, about that spider on the shed ...
You might still think it's a little creepy.

But isn't it
fascinating, too?

If you catch a spider
in a jar, be sure to let
it go when you're
done looking at it. It
has a lot of important
work to do!

Look Closely at a Spider

Look at a spider through a magnifying glass. How many of these different parts can you see?

- A spider's **jaws** are tipped with fangs.

- A spider uses its **pedipalps** to taste food.

- A spider's **eyes** see only light and dark.

- Each of a spider's eight **legs** has tiny claws on the tip.

- A spider lets out silk from its **spinnerets**.

cephalothorax
(joined head and thorax)

abdomen

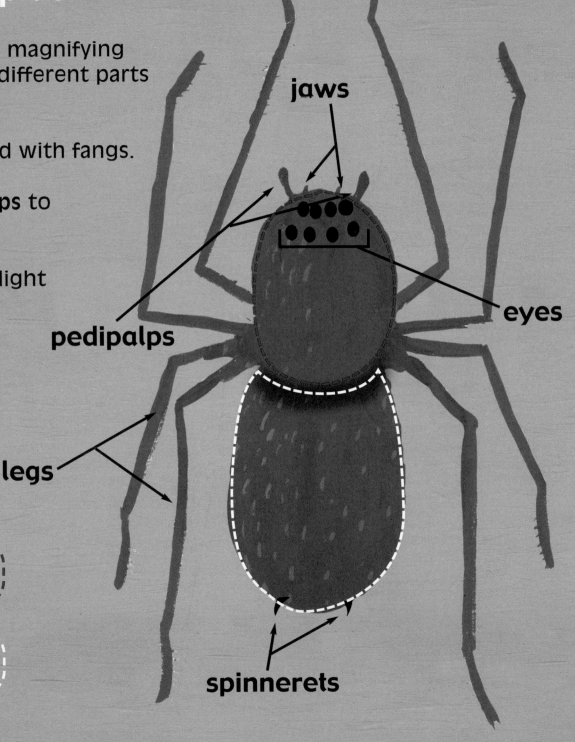

jaws

eyes

pedipalps

legs

spinnerets

Fun Facts

- Arachnophobia is a word that means "fear of spiders."

- Most spiders eat living prey, but some will eat bugs that are already dead.

- Spiders are great recyclers. When they need to make a new web, they eat the old one!

- Spiders don't crawl up through the pipes in your house. If you find a spider in a sink or bathtub, it probably went there looking for water and couldn't climb back up the smooth, slippery surface.

A Web of Your Own

Here's a fun way to make a spider web of your own. It's going to be messy, so spread a lot of old newspapers on the table.

Put a paper plate and a large piece of waxed paper on top of the newspapers. Have an adult help you cut a piece of string long enough to make a circle the size of the plate. Squirt out a bunch of glue onto the plate. Dip the string into the glue until it is completely covered. On the piece of waxed paper, make a circle with the string. That's the main part of your spider web.

Cut about 20 more pieces of string of different lengths, depending on what kind of pattern you want to create. Dip them in the glue and add them to your web.

Let your web dry overnight. The next day, carefully peel the waxed paper away. Make a spider out of paper, and glue it to your web.

Words to Know

abdomen – The abdomen is the last section of a bug's or spider's body.

digestive juices – Digestive juices are body liquids that break down food so that nutrients and energy can be used by the body.

mating – Mating spiders join together special parts of their bodies. After they've mated, the female spider can lay eggs.

paralyze – To paralyze another creature is to cause it to be unable to move.

prey – Animals that are hunted by other animals as food are called prey.

spiderlings – Spiderlings are baby spiders.

spinnerets – Spinnerets are parts on a spider's body that turn liquid silk into long threads.

venom – Venom is a poison that comes from the bite of an animal, such as a spider or snake. A spider's venom is stored in long, sharp teeth called fangs.

To Learn More

At the Library

Allen, Judy, and Tudor Humphries. *Are You a Spider?* New York: Kingfisher, 2000.

Birch, Robin. *Spiders Up Close.* Chicago: Raintree, 2005.

Platt, Richard. *Spiders' Secrets.* New York: Dorling Kindersley Publishing, 2001.

On the Web

FactHound offers a safe, fun way to find Web sites related to this book. All of the sites on FactHound have been researched by our staff. *www.facthound.com*

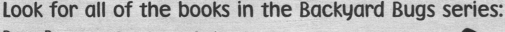

1. Visit the FactHound home page.
2. Enter a search word related to this book, or type in this special code: 1404811451.
3. Click on the FETCH IT button.

Your trusty FactHound will fetch the best sites for you!

Look for all of the books in the Backyard Bugs series:

Busy Buzzers: Bees in Your Backyard

Bzzz, Bzzz! Mosquitoes in Your Backyard

Chirp, Chirp! Crickets in Your Backyard

Dancing Dragons: Dragonflies in Your Backyard

Flying Colors: Butterflies in Your Backyard

Garden Wigglers: Earthworms in Your Backyard

Hungry Hoppers: Grasshoppers in Your Backyard

Living Lights: Fireflies in Your Backyard

Night Fliers: Moths in Your Backyard

Spotted Beetles: Ladybugs in Your Backyard

Tiny Workers: Ants in Your Backyard

Weaving Wonders: Spiders in Your Backyard

Index